MINE LIGHTHOUSE

Ready to Serve

E. Amoako

Codelitemedia

Copyright © 2024 Emmanuel Amoako

All rights reserved

All scripture quotations in this book are from the New King James Version of the Bible, with a few specified exceptions.

Keys for Other bible translations used:
KJV- King James Version
AMP- The Amplified Bible
NIV- New International Version

All Greek and Hebrew words and their definitions were picked from the Strongs and/or Thayer Bible Dictionaries.

Book design & Editing by: E. Amoako
email: codelitemedia@gmail.com
phone: 07856074470

I dedicate this book to all people of faith.

"You are the light of the world. A city set on a hill cannot be hidden; 15 nor does anyone light a lamp and put it under a basket, but on a lampstand, and it gives light to all who are in the house. 16 Let your light shine before men in such a way that they may see your good deeds and moral excellence, and glorify your Father who is in heaven".

MATT 5:14-16 AMP

ACKNOWLEDGEMENT

I am grateful for life, thanks be to the giver of days and the Source of all life. I extend heartfelt thanks to Pastor David F. Morgan for the kindness and gift of a 'big' bible. I have always dreamed of owning a large-sized bible so it is a dream come true. Words alone cannot fully express my appreciation for your generosity and kind-heartedness.

I thank Prophetess Regina Sarr, my diligent mother in the Lord who continually offer prayer support and direction. I also thank Rev.(Apostle) Wilfred Achumba and Pastor(Mrs.) Daphline Achumba for heeding God's call on their lives. A turning point in my christian walk was taking the school of ministry course offered at Elim Fountain of Hope. The outreach and support of the church in the community makes such great difference.

I also thank Rev. Arthur Janes, Minister Oldham Baptist Church for his kind service to the community. Thank you Stewart and Elizabeth Bailey for your magnanimity and support. I am very grateful to you all.

MINE LIGHTHOUSE

Ready to Serve

Who Are You?

Identity is a key part of our human lives. It tells that some identify as atheist, others vegans, some pacifist etc. Identity comes in the form of physical appearance (e.g. I'm underweight), profession (e.g. I'm a writer), emotions (e.g. I'm a considerate person) and sometimes by what we are not. (e.g. I'm not a smoker)

In Genesis 1:26, God said, **"Let Us make man in Our image, according to Our likeness...**

The deception in Gen 3: 5 was this, "God knows that when you eat of the tree, your eyes will be opened, **and you will be like God...**

Meanwhile God made the human according to His likeness- they were already, like God.

It has always been about identity, even from the beginning.

THE SOURCE OF ALL LIFE: THE SCRIPTWRITER

A script makes a good actor. An actor who win awards, or is described as talented, gifted, brilliant- is because they act their script right. The Scriptwriter set roles for the called out. (ecclesia) He assign them scripts with matching location. To be able to operate closest to our highest potential, one must find their place in God's kingdom agenda.

THE SCRIPTWRITER SET THE SCENE AND LOCATION

Imagine watching a two-hour long movie where the entire story unravels within the confines of a single room.

Not all scenes are set on the pulpit.

Location sets the mood, creates authenticity and immerses the audience in a movie's universe. Our heavenly Father places the people he calls, in different locations to play specific roles.

Some like Abraham will build altars and walk the land, engaging the transcendence. Gen 13:17 "Go, walk through the length and breadth of the land, for I am giving it to you."

Others like Joshua will engage the immanence and manifest divine destiny. "So Joshua took the entire land, just as the Lord had directed Moses". (Josh 11:23)

The marketplace Apostles, Prophets, Evangelists, Teachers and Pastors are placed strategically in commercial/secular settings, to bridge the gap between church (the institution) and everyday society.

In Acts 6, the twelve said, "It is not desirable that we should leave the word of God and serve tables". So seven people were selected to oversee the sharing of food.

It would seem these seven were handed the mundane, tending to the food and culinary needs of the everyday person. Now, among the seven was Philip. Fast forward to Acts 8, Philip was teleported from Gaza road to Azotus- such whirlwind encounters recorded probably only for Elijah and Jesus.

It is further recorded that, Philip went down to the city of Samaria and preached Christ to them. Unclean spirits came out of many who were possessed; many who were either lame or paralyzed were healed and the whole city rejoiced.

This is the power of service! When you serve, it open portals of knowledge, wisdom, understanding and renewal.

Philip also raised godly children. Acts 21:8,9 says Philip had four virtuous daughters who prophesied. Other early writings refer to Philip's daughters as great lights; luminaries that people travelled long distances to consult.

The importance of raising a godly family cannot be overemphasised. The testimony of God concerning Abraham (Gen

18:19kjv) was the stewardship of his household. The Lord found in him someone He could trust to raise a godly home- Abraham would teach His judgements, justice and counsel to his family and household. Through that stewardship, a mighty nation was going to come from Abraham and all nations of the earth was going to be blessed. This is how important a godly home is to the Lord.

Through service, Philip became a mighty man and all people benefited from the gifts and grace in the lives of his godly household.

This kind of service is not the routine, regimented coping mechanism. This one, unlock mysteries in the process of attempting to serve and fulfil an inspired assignment.

Do not make a shipwreck of your faith, clamouring for those seats on the high table. Was that not the sin of Lucifer?

May we find rest in the call of God as we identify our place in His eminent script, are you ready to serve?

CHAPTER 2

THE MARKETPLACE

Thesaurus defines marketplace as an open space, a place where ideas, thoughts, artistic creations, etc., compete for recognition; the world of commerce and exchange.

Christians are being sent to shine the light of God in our healthcare institutions, transport sector, military, music, sports, finance, in the councils and in every facet of everyday life. The power of darkness, is the absence of light. "Go into the world and preach the gospel to the whole creation", that is our commission. (Mk 16:15)

Unleash

This scripture in Ezekiel 19:9 comes to mind.

"They put him in a cage with chains, and brought him to the king of Babylon; they brought him in nets, that his voice should no longer be heard on the mountains of Israel".

In Luke 8:26-39, there was this man of Gadarene, who was kept under guard, bound with chains and shackles. He had been made homeless, driven into the wilderness and lived in tombs.

After his encounter with Jesus, where He set him free, he went his way and proclaimed throughout the whole city, in Decapolis all that Jesus had done for him; and all were in awe.

The chains were so that his voice would not be heard on the mountains of Decapolis; in the corridors of power and influence, in high places, in the market square. Any life in a cage, in chains, in a net, or that is tormented is because of their great commission, divine destiny and assignment.

The church is persecuted and often under attack because of our great commission and destiny. We are on assignment. But may we unleash and make our voices heard on the mountains and to the ends of the earth.

Further reading: (Mk 16:15, Lk 14:23, Matt 28:19-20, Acts 1:7-8)

3- TYPES OF MINISTRY BY LOCATION

1. Altar Ministry
2. Pulpit Ministry
3. Marketplace Ministry

Explaining The Types Of Ministry By Location

A church institution like the Catholic Church run schools. These schools are normally open to all members of society irrespective of faith or creed. Their schools and hospitals comprise their marketplace ministry.

The monks, nuns/ sisters and the wholly devoted make the altar ministry arm, the Church/Parish officialdom make the pulpit ministry.

Altar Ministry

The Altar ministry serves as the backend of the church infrastructure. They mostly comprise seers, prophets, intercessors, nuns, monks, wholly devoted men and women. They tend to be reclusive and lead much more enclosed lives.

Much of science was pioneered by monks, priests and devout laypersons who described themselves as 'thinking God's thoughts after Him'. Nicolaus Copernicus was a Catholic canon. (formulated that the Sun, instead of the earth was at the center of the solar system) Joseph Priestly was an English theologian. (credited with his independent discovery of oxygen) Gregor Mendel was an Austrian monk (whose work with peas led to the discovery of hereditary pattern of traits) to name but a few.

Pulpit Ministry

Pulpit Ministry is the mainstream church institution. They keep the sanctity of the church system. They govern the church. Example the Pope, cardinals, episcopal council etc.

Marketplace Ministry

Marketplace Ministry is the link between mainstream church and everyday society. This is what James would term, show me your faith without works and I will show you my faith by my works. The called to the marketplace show their faith by deed.

An example of someone in the bible placed in the marketplace is Daniel. Bible scholars regard him as a major Prophet. He served in the courts of King Nebuchadnezzar. During that time, he was made ruler over the entire province of Babylon and put in charge of all its wise men.

When others were been served food and wine from the King's table, Daniel requested for 'vegetarian portions' and water. When he was examined after ten days, it is recorded that he appeared better looking and more nourished than the rest that ate from the King's table.

>Daniel's kind of faith was practical; faith by works.

Daniel was also an important intercessor (Dan 9).

In Ezekiel 14:20, he is mentioned alongside patriarchs Noah and Job, as examples of great people trusted to uphold righteousness in their generation. Jesus himself confirms Daniel as a prophet of great importance (Matt 24:15). He validates Daniel's end time prophecies.

◆ ◆ ◆

Daniel was a Prophet placed in the marketplace, unlike Samuel who ministered to the Lord in the tabernacle(pulpit ministry) as a priest, prophet and judge.

Those called to the marketplace mostly operate in one or several of the anointing of the 7-Spirits of God. (Is11:2,3)

One's placement in the marketplace (example advisor to Kings, as seen in the case of Daniel), is not a result of their level of spiritual gifting, talents or ability per se. It is the Scriptwriter who decides who serves where.

THE SEVEN SPIRITS OF GOD (REV 4:5)

1. The Spirit of the Lord (lordship, leadership, authority, monarchs etc.)

2. The Spirit of Wisdom (law, adjudicators etc.)

3. The Spirit of Understanding (interpreters of dreams, analysts, philosophers etc.)

4. The Spirit of Counsel (advisors, consultants etc.)

5. The Spirit of Power (legislators, financiers etc.)

6. The Spirit of Knowledge (research, inventions, academia etc.)

7. The Spirit of the Fear of the Lord (ethical, conscientious)

In this book, we would examine seven mighty men and women who were called to the marketplace.

CHAPTER 3

GIDEON

Much of the account of Gideon is recorded in the book of Judges. The Talmud ascribes the writer to Samuel who is recorded in the bible as a writer. 1Sam 10:25
The children of Israel again did evil in the sight of The Lord and so were delivered into the hands of Midian for seven years. At the time, they hid in caves, tunnels, dens and strongholds in the mountains.

The Midianites were descendants of Midian, a son of Abraham and Keturah, a nomadic people who lived east of the Jordan River and the Dead Sea. The Amalekites were located in the Negev and the Sinai Peninsula. The Amalekites however descended from Esau's grandson Amalek.

While doing an everyday chore threshing wheat, Gideon had an encounter with an Angel. He was commissioned to rescue the children of Israel in his might.

After a couple of confirmations that divine help is been made available, Gideon gathered 32, 000 fighters. Through a series of tests occasioned by the Lord, the number whittled down to 300. With these three hundred men, victory was secured over the Midianite coalition numbering over 120,000 (Jgs 8:10).

GIDEON'S CALL TO THE MARKETPLACE

Gideon appears in the period before the rise of the monarchy in Israel. There were Judges chosen by the Lord and anointed with

His Spirit. These Judges were Civil and Military Leaders. Gideon is classed as a major judge who led Israel in the conquest of Midian.

After Midian was subdued, Israel enjoyed peace for forty years in the days of Gideon.

THE TOP 1%

According to a 2021 credit suisse report, the top 1% of the world's population holds more than 45% of global wealth.

A study by the Swiss Federal Institute of Technology(SFIT) found that 147 companies controlled nearly 40% of the global economy.

The richest one percent made nearly two-thirds of all new wealth worth $42 trillion created since 2020, Oxfam report.

In the search engine industry one company, Google, had a market share of around 96% on smartphones as of 2022 according to data from Statcounter.

Just two companies, Netflix and Amazon Prime Video make up approximately 40-42% of the global streaming service market.

The top 1% often serve as gatekeepers in the Arts, funding and promoting specific artists and movements. This patronage shapes the cultural landscape, determining which art receives visibility and acclaim. They are the primary buyers in the high-end art market, significantly influencing art trends and valuations. In 2019, just 1% of artists accounted for 64% of the total sales in the art market

The Getty family, for example, has had a huge impact on the art world through the Getty Museum and its extensive acquisitions and exhibitions.

GIDEON'S 1%

Out of the 32,000 people Gideon gathered, 300 were chosen. It was with this 300 that Midian was subdued.

300/32,000 x 100% will make 0.937, approximately 1%.

A one percent that drinks water while holding their weapons.

A 1% that drink of the Lord (John 7:37), with a frontline mind set. Those that would combine the celestial and the terrestrial. Those who will bring the kingdom of God on earth.

Your kingdom come, your will be done on earth as it is in heaven. (Matt 6:10)

The battleground is the marketplace, occupy till I come, says the Lord.

◆ ◆ ◆

Jesus did not put up a single church building; He empowered the twelve. The Holy Spirit filled the about one hundred and twenty in the upper room. The Father sent One, the Son.

> *Today nearly 2.4 billion people identify as Christians, according to Pew Research.*

The ways of the Godhead, even appear to suggest quality to quantity.

We do not need more Christians to make global impact. We need a willing, courageous, proactive, deliberate and versatile 1% to change our world.

TRACK RECORD

Christians have led the transformation of our world in different fields.

Science came about in the West because of the Christian belief in creation's uniformity and predictability as opposed to animistic chaos and capricious polytheism. And as opposed to Islamic determinism or pantheistic spiritualization of nature.

Christianity convinced the Greco-Roman and Barbarian worlds that all people are made in the image of God and therefore rightful objects of charity as Christ commanded, saving the weak and vulnerable in a class society.

Christians view their work as an extension of their faith and a vocation from God--seen in the numerous Christian hospitals, schools and organisations around the world.

CALL TO AMBIDEXTERITY

The Vatican, the administrative and spiritual center of the Catholic Church, maintains diplomatic relations with 183 countries. This unique status as both a religious and political entity allows the Catholic Church to exert significant influence on global affairs.

The Catholic Church's position on social issues, such as poverty, human rights, and bioethics are highly influential. Encyclicals and other teachings from the Pope often shape public discourse and policy debates on moral and ethical matters worldwide.

The Apostolic church is a church that is sent out, a people sent to a dark world to bring light.

You can be a part of Gideon's 1%, and make a difference wherever your location. Whether you serve in Government, Finance, Healthcare, in the Council or in the Police service.

CHARACTERISTICS OF GIDEON'S 1%

Desire

There are many people who would like to see godly values and virtues permeate our schools, housing associations, media etc. They want to see righteous judgements from the Supreme Courts and from the judiciary. For Moses to be called by the Angel during the burning bush encounter, he had to be curious and interested in that extraordinary phenomenon. It was when he showed interest and got nearer the burning bush in inquisitiveness, that he had the call. The manner of questions Gideon asked the Angel implied he was concerned about the plight of his people. The 32,000 who responded to Gideon's invitation have shown a desire and a willingness to confront the Midian challenge. It is a good starting place.

Courage

Those who were afraid of the task, were asked to go home. Fear is contagious, just as courage.

True courage is rooted in conviction. It is about standing firm in our beliefs, even when it is unpopular or difficult.

Courage comes in many forms. It can be the whistle blower who exposes corruption, or the individual who simply speaks the truth in the face of opposition. It can also be found in everyday acts of kindness and integrity, such as the student who stands against bullying.

Proactive

The third attribute devised to separate the 300 from the lot was their tactfulness and proactivity. Dropping their weapons while drinking was dropping guard. The 1% are people who would not be taken by surprise.

To be proactive means to take initiative, to anticipate challenges, and to act before circumstances compel one to do so. It is about taking control of our lives, setting goals, and working towards them with determination and foresight.

◆ ◆ ◆

Instead of waiting for opportunities to come to us, we create them. Instead of reacting to problems as they arise, we anticipate and prevent them.

I like this story of the man healed at the pool called Bethesda (in John 5). An angel would come at a certain time to stir the water. Gathered around the pool were scores of sick people. Whoever stepped in first after the stirring was healed of whatever disease.

Jesus came to the water and healed this man who was there, thirty-eight years with infirmity. The angel had not come; the water was not stirring but Jesus brought healing to the man. That is the grace called Apostleship. It carries solution to situations, instead of hoping that somehow there would be a lucky dip. It is possible to be caught up in a cycle of the miraculous and interventions, it is not sustainable. The best form of defense is attack.

Holy Spirit Led

In Judges 6:34, The Spirit of the Lord would come upon Gideon. The Hebrew translation says, "The Spirit of the Lord clothed Himself with Gideon". The Holy Spirit is our advantage and if we are to be successful envoys and ambassadors of our Lord, then we must cultivate a healthy relationship with the Helper. (Jn 14:26)

It is not enough to have the desire or willingness to see the advancement of God's kingdom on earth. It is still not enough to be courageous.

A combination of desire, boldness, tact and being Holy Spirit led is what is required to be in this 1%.

By the 300, I will save you and deliver the Midianites into your hand!

ACHIEVING MORE WITH LESS: GIDEON-STRATEGY

Charity Begins At Home

The first step to achieving more with less is prioritising what truly matters.

For Gideon it was the elimination of household altars. Your body is a temple, it is the home of the Holy Spirit. My being is the first home.

For the Holy Spirit to have maximum impact in my life, competing spirits must be shut out. This reduces the habit of having to discern two, three voices within. *There are ways to cut oneself from fountains that are not of the Holy Spirit.* (A Prophet, Seer or Apostle well versed in the area of deliverance can guide you through the process of disconnecting from covenants running in the family pedigree that are not divine).

Achieving more with less also means taking care of your nutritional needs. It is an inside out process.

Start with you, your household, your community and then to the nations.

Charity begins at home means self-preservation and self-compassion. I have to be alive, in order to be able to envisage aspiration. Gideon preserved his life by threshing wheat in a winepress. Sometimes premature exposure could be dangerous for us and our divine assignments. There can be a Cave of Adullam period (1 Sam 22), a time where one is preserved, groomed and made ready for their future assignments.

Code Cracking & Spiritual Homeopathy

In the fictional story of The Sleeping Beauty, the way to break the spell of Maleficent was the Princess finding true love. Many obstacles were put in the way of the Prince so he would not come to find the Princess.

There are ways like that in the supernatural. Sometimes there are set ways or formula to break bleeding cases, called code cracking.

The Midianites prevailed against the children of Israel for *seven* years, and Gideon had to make a burnt sacrifice with the second bull of *seven* years old.

Sometimes the way to solve prolonged, long standing issues and situations come by way of code cracking or spiritual directions.

Spiritual homeopathy is a like-for-like kind of code cracking. Moses was asked to raise a bronze serpent when the children of Israel were been bitten by serpents in the wilderness. When Adam and Eve ate their way into sin, Jesus also gave the communion.

Further reading: (Num 21:8, Matt 26:26)

Delegate And Collaborate

Don't be afraid to delegate tasks to others or collaborate with others. By leveraging the strengths and expertise of those around us, one can achieve more without having to do everything themselves. Gideon divided his team into three companies, tasking each group with specific duties.

Look for ways to streamline the chain of command and reduce complexity and bureaucracy. Gideon gave clear instructions and simplified the task.

"My yoke is easy and my burden is light" (Matt 11:28-30).

By prioritising, self-care, delegating, collaborating and divine help, one can maximise effectiveness and achieve goals with fewer resources.

CHAPTER 4

NICODEMUS

The name Nicodemus in Greek means "Conqueror of the People"

Nicodemus was a Pharisee, a member of the Jewish Ruling Council (the Sanhedrin)-a teacher of Israel. As a Pharisee, he was thoroughly trained in Jewish law and theology. He came to Jesus at night for a conversation. It is from that dialogue that we have the all-time popular Christian bible quotation (John 3:16), For God so loved the world...

He continues in his position in the Council and when it matters most, he defends Jesus among his Pharisee peers arguing that Jesus is not guilty, until He is granted a fair hearing.

Nicodemus reappears after the death of Jesus and brings myrrh and aloes measuring about a hundred pounds for the burial of Jesus in accordance with Jewish custom.

(Jn 3:1-21, Jn 7:50-52, Jn 19:39-42)

NICODEMUS' CALL TO THE MARKETPLACE

There are a certain group of people called to the Judiciary, the Courts, the Diplomatic corps, the Secret services and other delicate sectors. By way of the sensitive nature of these roles, jobs or vocation the chosen ones sent to these spaces are circumspect of their public utterances and associations. This would show in how Nicodemus comes to Jesus under the cover of night. However, these people have been strategically placed in these locations and would rise to the challenge at the appointed time. When Elijah proferred he was the only one standing for righteousness, the Lord said to him there are 7000 in Israel who have not bowed to Baal or kissed him. Kingdom work is not a craft set in showmanship. It is one that entails a very deep, clever, multifaceted architecture.

Satan used the serpent who was more cunning than any field creature the Lord had made. If Satan uses intelligence, how much more the Creator. God would use super intelligence and superior thinking. Those that come by day are welcome; those who come by night are also welcome.

Further reading: (1 Kgs 19:18, Gen 3:1)

LESSONS FROM NICODEMUS

Took His Destiny Into His Own Hands

Nicodemus did not follow the crowd; he took responsibility for himself. Despite being a member of the Sanhedrin and surrounded by people who opposed Jesus, he himself believed.

Follow your own life's blueprint. Do not conform, but be transformed.

Nicodemus Was Calculated

Nicodemus was bold to speak up for Jesus. He opined He was entitled to a fair hearing. Found mostly guilty in the court of public opinion, (Example the public would rather Barabbas be released instead of Jesus) Jesus would need this intervention.

Time Such As This

I borrow this phrase from Mordecai as recorded in the book of Esther. When it was time to show up, Nicodemus acted in a way that made his faith public. At the time when Jesus' twelve disciples were scattered, some denying Him Nicodemus rose up to the occasion. He together with Joseph of Arimathea took the body of Jesus and gave him a befitting Jewish burial. It is not about how you start that matters, it is how you finish.

YOU MUST BE BORN AGAIN

Redemption is not the same as being born again. The Greek word translated as redeem is *agorazo.* It means to make market of opportunity, to haunt the market. While we were still sinners, God could see an opportunity in us to become born again. Redemption in essence is an investment.

We are redeemed by the token of his death and born again by engaging His resurrection. Redemption is the starting place, being born again and experiencing the power of resurrection is the full package of salvation.

For the joy that was set before him Jesus endured the cross, despising the shame. What was the joy? The joy was that He would bring many sons and daughters into glory, through His resurrection.

Joint resurrection, is what avails unto a new creation in Christ. This is how the new creation is attained.

You are not born again because you stopped doing bad things. Atheists do good things; humanists practise good neighbourliness. Other religions practice generosity and charity.

You are not born again because you go to church either. It was the chief priests, the scribes and the elders of the people who plotted to kill Jesus.

Right Believing

Muslims believe in Jesus, as one of the prophets. There are other religions and occult fraternities who believe in Master Jesus.

God gave his only begotten Son, that whosoever believes in him should not perish.

Does only believing that Jesus is a prophet or a Master grant everlasting life?

It is not just believing in Jesus, it is the right believing of Him. The content of your belief is what gets you born again or not. When the content of your belief is wrong, the premise or foundation of your new birth is defective and therefore ineffectual.

The death of Jesus fulfils the demands for the forgiveness of sins. His resurrection is what gets one born again! I revisit being born again in chapter ten, *Episterizo*.

Further reading: (Heb 9:12, Heb 12:2, 1 Pt 1:3, 1 Corin 15:17-18, Rom 6:4, Rom 10:9, Col 3:1, Phil 3:10, Matt 26:3-5)

SPECIAL DUTIES

It was divine instruction that Moses send out 12 people, (among them Joshua who succeeded him) to spy the land of Canaan.

There is a section of the ecclesia sent to places to gather intelligence and information. They would act like them, speak like them, play like them but they are not of them. We are in the world but not of the world.

Take for instance an evangelist who was an ex-offender or addict. By the time they are drawn to Christ, they know how to reach those in similar situations and circumstances because they have been there and they understand. Saul after his encounter became the Apostle Paul. Likewise, some people have been sent to bring information to the body and to save lives. It is easier when an investment banker speaks to his colleague banker about Jesus, when a squaddie speaks to his fellow soldier. Way easier when a member of parliament evangelises to a fellow MP.

His ways are not our ways, and His thoughts our thoughts.

Further reading: (Num 13, Jn 15:19, Is 55:8,9)

INSIDERS

David's life was spared on account of Jonathan speaking well of him to his father, Saul the King. Jonathan was an insider, who would relay relevant information. Saul's daughter Michal, David's wife, also saved David's life on at least one occasion.

Michal let David down a window, to escape from Saul's messengers who had come to seize and hand him over to be killed.

These insiders and informants are strategically placed to do divine bidding and abort ungodly plans.

For example, a section of society believe the Covid-19 pandemic was a biological laboratory leak. Granted that was the case, could there not be people of faith working in such places as laboratory scientists who are there to uphold justice and righteousness, to save lives?

No part of the world is out of reach for the Creator of the world. Everyone's calling is unique. Find your own location and purpose. Originality comes from *origin*. Connect to the Source, the One who knows your place and location.

Further reading: (1 Sam 19, 2 Sam 1:11-16)

RIGHTEOUS AMONG THE NATIONS

Yad Vashem was set up in 1963 and is chaired by a Justice of the Supreme Court of Israel. It is the body tasked with conferring the honorary title *Righteous Among the Nations* on individuals, diplomats, civil servants etc. who assisted Jews to escape the holocaust.

As at the beginning of 2022, around 28, 000 men and women from over 50 countries have been officially recognised as helping Jews escape the holocaust.

A story I extracted from the times of Israel newspaper records the effort of one recipient of the honorary title. The recipient, H. Kleinicke, had joined the Nazi party in 1933. He took advantage of his position, as a chief officer in charge of construction in a town called Silesia to save countless lives. What he did was to 'claim Jews' as workers. These workers were granted certificates that they work for Kleinicke. Survivors claim with this certificate they were treated like V.I.P.'s, exempted.

His direct intervention reportedly rescued around a 100 people. Kleinicke, aside this is thought to have sheltered Jews in his basement, particularly those at risk of deportation to Auschwitz (just over 10 miles away from Silesia). He also alerted Jews about upcoming roundups.

Stories like this show that there would be people like Nicodemus, a Pharisee and in the Sanhedrin, they would come at night. But they would uphold righteousness, justice and truth. They have been placed purposely, to save lives.

CHAPTER 5

JOSEPH OF ARIMATHEA

The story of Joseph of Arimathea appear in all four gospels. Joseph of Arimathea was a wealthy disciple of Jesus. He came from Arimathea in Judea and hence the designation.

He was a good and just man who managed to both be a member of the Jewish Ruling Council (the Sanhedrin) and a follower of Jesus. The bible records that he disagreed with the Council's decisions and actions against Jesus.

After the death of Jesus, he requested to take Jesus' body for proper burial in accordance with Jewish custom. He went to Pilate (the Roman governor of Judaea under emperor Tiberius) to make that demand. Permission was granted and the body was taken down. Joseph, with the help of Nicodemus, wrapped Jesus' body in clothes and spices. Jesus was buried in a tomb that Joseph may have intended for himself.

Further reading: (Matt 27:57-60, Mk 15:42-64, Lk 23:50-53, Jn 19:38-42).

JOSEPH'S CALL TO THE MARKETPLACE

There are people who are called to enterprise, entrepreneurship and wealth creation; kingdom financiers. Joseph is described as wealthy and influential. He was a prominent member of the Jewish Ruling Council, which was both a judicial and administrative body for Jews.

LESSONS FROM JOSEPH OF ARIMATHEA

Courage

Mark writes in his gospel account of the death of Jesus, that it was a bold action for Joseph to request for the body of Jesus from Pilate. Mark points this out because at that time public association with Jesus had become risky. The unfavourable atmosphere shows in the denial of Jesus by Peter and the fact that most of the other Apostles were not to be found around Golgotha, at the time of Jesus' death.

Devoted

Joseph risked his own life. He put his wealth, business and sprawling estate on the line to do this work for our Lord and saviour. Being a member of the Sanhedrin, Joseph was surrounded by Jesus' antagonist, but he was awaiting the kingdom of God and he believed.

Influential

Joseph is described as a prominent member of the Council. It is said that he distinguished himself among his peers, playing a key role in the council's affairs.

All the above are also traits of highly successful people. They are risk takers, courageous, they chart their own paths and are industrious.

KINGDOM FINANCIERS

I wish above all things that, you may prosper and be in health as your soul also prospers. (3 Jn 2)

There are people called to kingdom financing. Luke mentions Mary called Magdalene, Joanna the wife of Chuza and Susanna as people who provided financial support for Jesus. These women were with Jesus to the end. When He had risen from the dead, the first people to see Him included His financiers; Mary Magdalene and Joanna. What a privilege to partner with Jesus.

Aquila and Priscilla offered accommodation and work placement in their tent making business for Paul at Corinth.

There was a Shunammite woman described as wealthy, who would provide meals for Prophet Elisha. She also prepared a spare room in their house for him.

It is not all who would mount pulpits, stages and prayer mountains, there are certain people called specially to the area of financial partnership, financing and wealth creation.

Further reading: (Lk 8:1-3, 24:8-10, 2 Kgs 4:8)

THE EARTH IS THE LORD'S AND THE FULLNESS THEREOF (PS 24:1)

Christians In Charity & Philanthropy

There would be people who are called to the area of kind acts and charity. Dorcas whom Peter raised from death, was known to be full of good works. She would assist those in need providing clothing and tunic. (Acts 9:36-43)

Christians In Banking & Finance

Stocks, forex, commodities and indices trading are a great source of wealth creation for Christians. Investment banking is another. According to a study by Glassdor, the average salary for a forex trader in London is about £154,000 per annum. They earn significant bonuses. Worldwide equity trading surpassed $100 trillion in 2023(Statista report).

Christians in I.T. and Computing

It is a digital era and Christians are encouraged to explore this source of wealth. NVIDIA, a designer and supplier of graphic cards for video games and a leader in chips for Artificial intelligence, reported earnings of over $40 billion in 2023. The company's market capital crossed $1 trillion in mid-2023, by march 2024 the market capital was $2 trillion, hitting $3 trillion in June 2024. There is such quantum growth and potential in this sector.

Christians In Enterprise

Extra streams of income offer a reliable path to wealth creation, be it passive or active income sources. Christians are encouraged to explore options for multiple streams of income.

Christians In Property & Land Acquisition

Property is an integrated sector comprising services in areas such as legal, finance and management. With global population increase and dwindling resources, real estate and land offer an avenue for steady revenue and long term investment opportunity for Christians.

SOLOMON'S WEALTH

Ask for whatever you want me to give you

In a night vision, King Solomon was given a blank cheque, "ask for whatever you want me to give you". In the vision, Solomon requested for understanding and wisdom.

The answer he gave pleased the Lord and He said to offer him things that Solomon did not ask for, among them wealth and honour. The Lord gives wealth and honour.

Jesus Himself talks about the splendour of Solomon and his wealth, juxtaposing it with the lilies of the field in Matthew's gospel.

It is said that King Solomon was greater in riches and wisdom than all other kings in his time. He answered all the hard questions Queen Sheba brought to test him. Nothing was too hard for Solomon to explain to her. King Solomon's dining cups were made of gold, and all the household articles in the Palace were pure gold. Nothing was made of silver, because silver was considered of little value in the house of Solomon.

Further reading: (1 Kgs 3: 5-15, 1 Kgs 10:14-25, 27, Matt 6:29)

PRAYER OF JABEZ

Jabez prayed for increase, and God granted his request.
Further reading: (1 Chro 4:10)

CHAPTER 6

NAOMI

The story of Naomi is found in the book of Ruth. Jewish tradition ascribes the writer to Samuel. Ruth occurs during the period of the Judges, as a part of those events that occur between the death of Joshua and the rise of Samuel's influence. In Hebrew, Naomi means Pleasant, Delightful, Lovely.

Naomi lived in Judah with her husband Elimelech. During a famine in Judah, Naomi, her husband and their two sons relocated to Moab. Her sons were Mahlon and Chilion.

At Moab tragedy struck, Elimelech passed away. Both her sons died too, leaving Naomi to make her way back to Bethlehem. She had heard from Moab that the famine was over, that there was now bread in Judah.

Her surviving daughters in law were Ruth and Orpah. She bid them farewell, asking each to return to their own families. However, one of them Ruth, insisted she would go with Naomi. She pleaded that Naomi's people become her people and Naomi's God her God. This was a commitment to stick by Naomi and to journey with her.

Naomi returns to Bethlehem to a rousing welcome. She seemed to be loved by her people and by all her associates, a pleasant person just as her name suggested.

She blamed God for her predicament, further adding she had gone to Moab full, only to return empty. It was the beginning of barley harvest season in Bethlehem, when she returned.

NAOMI'S CALL TO THE MARKETPLACE

Naomi seemed to have been strategically placed to advance God's master plan of salvation on earth. Naomi connecting Ruth to Boaz physically produced Obed, the grandfather of David. Spiritually heralding the commonwealth of nations in Christ, Jew or Gentile in the Messianic lineage.

Naomi's call to the marketplace can be found in the area of family restoration, mentorship, child adoption and family services. It is recorded that Naomi became a nurse to Obed and it was said, there is a son born to Naomi.

There is a call to restore family values, heal troubled homes, mend broken hearts and safeguard wounded children.

CALL ME MARA

Mara in Hebrew means bitter. Naomi asked to be called bitter, because she thought her life had been bitter. But what does the much liked paradox of 'bitter' tell us.

> When milk turns bitter, it becomes yoghurt. Yoghurt is of more value than milk. Cheese is as sour as one gets stale milk. Cheese is more expensive than both yoghurt and milk.

When corn gets biting, it turns to whisky. Whisky is exotic and much more expensive than corn. When grape juice turns sour, it becomes wine. Wine is pricier than grape juice.

Be it yoghurt, whisky, wine, or cheese, the break down process makes them better than their original form. God would mess up your makeup, to make up your mess.

Your setback can be a setup for your comeback.

In God you become better rather than bitter, vintage not old.

What Naomi thought was bitter, became a set up for generational blessing and enduring legacy. Call me Mara!

RUTH: THE TYPICAL PROVERBS 31 WOMAN

The narrative of King Lemuel in Proverbs 31:10-31 of a virtuous woman, so aptly describes Ruth. Ruth was a virtuous woman, Boaz affirms. She was hardworking and she was steadfast in her devotion to Naomi. God chooses people based on the condition of their hearts. This is what He said to Prophet Samuel when he had gone to the house of Jesse to anoint King Saul's replacement, which happened to be David. Human beings look at the outward appearance, nationality, social standing etc., God looks at the heart. Ruth was chosen among all people to perpetuate Messianic lineage and that tells in her values; the condition of her heart.

MENTORING RUTH

It is interesting how the book is named after Naomi's mentee Ruth. It seems as though Ruth takes prominence and becomes more notable. However, there is a Naomi behind the scene.

That should be the goal of mentorship. The mentee should accomplish more and reach heights that sometimes the mentor has not trodden. Jethro is a very quiet figure in the bible, but his mentee, a runaway fugitive called Moses is one of the most important Prophets in the Judeo Christian faith. There is the Abrahamic Covenant and there is the Mosaic Covenant. Jethro occupies a quiet place in scripture, but he is so influential in the life of Moses. His well-trained and knowledgeable daughter Zipporah, (Moses 'wife) would save Moses from imminent death. She cut the foreskin of their son and put the blood on Moses feet, to ward of death. Jethro would also counsel Moses to appoint leaders to assist him. This happens at a time Moses was mounting an unsustainable spiritual highway that could have led to his premature demise. Moses had evolved from a tempestuous killer, to become the meekest man that lived on the face of the earth.

And that is how most of God's mighty Generals are called to be; to offer invaluable tutelage, advice and direction. It is not really about fame and the spotlight. Naomi was God's General in her generation, with a great commission. She suffered unprecedented mishaps and calamity in lieu of that assignment. However, none would stop this great matriarch from fulfilling purpose.

Further reading: (Exodus 4:24-26, Num 12:3)

ENTREAT ME NOT TO LEAVE YOU

This rather poetic and elegant statement attributed to Ruth, was Ruth saying to Naomi that I would trod where you trod and go where you go; entreat me not to leave you.

It seems there was a spark in Ruth to stick by Naomi.

In mentoring, normally you expose the mentee to what's on offer and see what draws them.

It is the responsibility of the mentee to make the best of the opportunities on offer. Jesus did not heal all who were sick. He walked pass a blind man. He did stop because, he who was blind screamed and shouted for His attention. Calling Him son of David, he pleaded for mercy. It was only then Jesus attended to him, restoring his sight.

You must desire, want and sometimes contend for what's on offer.

❖ ❖ ❖

When Samuel lived in the house of Eli (the High Priest), Eli's children were being wayward. Living under that same roof in the same environment, Samuel was having divine encounters.

> It is not about the crowd or what the majority is doing.
> It is about running your own race and running with discipline.

Through focus and commitment to his own destiny, it is said that none of Samuel's words fell to the ground. He became a mighty Prophet anointing as Kings of Israel, Saul and David and writing several books of the bible. He was honourable.

Ruth pursued a righteous path, and ended up with a generational blessing.

GENERATIONAL BLESSINGS

Ruth teaches how generational blessings are constructed or initiated. In Ruth's case, it involved a process of calamity, determination, guidance and eventual success.

There are generational blessings of wealth, health, possessions, positions (as in a royal lineage, /Monarchs).

Whiles all of these are good, spiritual generational blessings come first. It is best to connect to the Source of all blessing. The silver and gold is the Lord's. (Haggai 2:8)

Ruth saw the need to make the God of Israel her God, closing the old fountains of Moab and connecting to a new fountain of the Lord God of Israel.

I LIVED TO TELL THE TALE

From numerous research and keen observation, I have come to a firm understanding that great destinies attract battles. Remember, just about when Moses was born there was a command from the Pharaoh (King of Egypt) to kill all male children.

At the birth of Jesus, all male children in Bethlehem and all its districts, from two years old and under were massacred.

Esther lost both parents at a young age. She was an orphan.

The devil comes not, but to steal, kill and destroy. Moses and Jesus made divine escapes, evading the wiles of the enemy to fulfil their lives' purpose.

In the case of Naomi, I see that same tactic been deployed to wipe out the entire family. The enemy devised to thwart a divine agenda. Out of the four that travelled to Moab, 75% were taken out. All but one survives.

◆ ◆ ◆

Naomi in retrospect would see that her survival was a miraculous escape. As happened for Moses, Jesus and Esther, Naomi survives to tell a tale. Whenever such great salvation occur, it points to an unfinished business, that there is more, there is a great next chapter.

This phenomenon permeate scripture. Daniel miraculously escaped the lion's den. It was after this great escape that Daniel recorded the vision of the four beasts, the vision of the Ancient of Days, his encounter with Angel Gabriel, his prayer for his people that 70 years of desolation is accomplished etc. There was so much in store for Daniel.

Most of the other Apostles got martyred, when it got to the turn of John he spectacularly escaped a cauldron of burning oil.

He was then exiled to prison on the island of Patmos. He later fled to Ephesus. The book of the Revelation of Jesus Christ was written within that period of exile. Therein the letters to the seven churches, the seven seals, the seven signs etc. The book of the revelation of Jesus Christ is often the most important resource in Christian eschatology.

When you have survived something that could or should easily have killed you, or destroyed others but you pull through, it is a telltale sign and significant indication that there is unfinished business. It is a sign, you are still on God's radar. It does not matter the age, as was the case with Naomi and also Elizabeth (the mother of John, the Baptist). The name of the Lord was blessed because of Naomi, He proved Himself able in her life. Naomi survives to tell the tale.

Further reading: (Dan 6-12, Lk 1:5-25, 39-80)

NAOMI ATTRIBUTES

Naomi Was Transparent

Naomi would not hide her struggles. It is a good thing to be open about one's misgivings, shortcomings and the lack of intelligibility of some of life's outcomes.

In the book of Job, he expresses frustration, pain and discomfort in his unprecedented tragedies and misfortunes. He got answers at the appointed time and he was restored.

One key value I have learnt on my faith journey is to be transparent and honest about issues. In that way, I have both received solution and counsel from people and from above.

Naomi Kept Her Faith

Naomi did not abandon her faith, even in a foreign land. She lived among idol worshipers yet she did not renounce her faith. Ruth wanted Naomi's God to be her God. This is not taken lightly considering, many great people faltered in this way. Solomon turned away from the God of Israel and pursued foreign gods in his later years. Following strange foreign gods was always a great snare to the children of Israel. Naomi kept the faith.

Naomi Was Very Discerning

Naomi knew when to move away from Moab. Sometimes when things are not working, we must discern the signs and times and act accordingly. She could also tell Ruth was determined to go with her so she budged. Back in Judah, when she realised that Ruth had unknowingly walked into Boaz's field, she figured it was not coincidence. Soon afterward she would guide Ruth on what next steps to take to be redeemed. All these moments of decision she got right, show how discerning and spiritually astute Naomi was.

Naomi Was Loving

Naomi had a good relationship with her daughters in law. She truly and genuinely cared for them. She did not portend entitlement, that they are to care for her as she was ageing. Instead she would go home to her own people. What selfless, humble, loving woman. She dealt honestly with her daughters in law, releasing them each to their own purpose and life's assignment.

Clothed In Wisdom

Naomi was well versed in the customs, rites and the ways of her people. Not one of her insightful counsel to Ruth fell to the ground. Those called to the marketplace would have the knack for practical intelligence and godly wisdom.

CHAPTER 7

ESTHER

Esther is a study in the survival and the thriving of God's people in a time of animosity. The King's most senior officer, Haman wants the Jews destroyed. King Ahasuerus signs a decree for their execution under manipulation from Haman. Esther saves her people, through works of selflessness, humility, team work and a recognition that prayer can change things. By way of the marriage of practical, thoughtful, decisive steps and the supernatural, she achieves great deliverance for her people.

Born Hadassah, Esther was adopted by Mordecai after the death of her father and mother. She was an orphan.

Her Hebrew name Hadassah, occurs only once in the bible. There is scholarly consensus that it is the feminine of *hadas,* meaning myrtle. In Zechariah 1:11, an Angel of the Lord, is mentioned stood among myrtle trees. Little wonder, Esther carried divine presence, manifest as favour.

She is initially described as lovely and beautiful. Later it is discovered that behind that beauty laid a prayerful, purposeful, wise and selfless person.

The narrative is found in the book of Esther and the story takes place over a period of four years. The book of Esther is the only book in the biblical canon that does not mention God by name. This fit perfectly with how God works behind the scenes, through the faith, wisdom and the courage of strategically placed people in the marketplace.

ESTHER'S CALL TO THE MARKETPLACE

Esther became the queen of the Persian King Ahasuerus. Esther was called to the area of rule and governance. She started that journey from the arena of cosmetics, beauty and fashion. Some would be sent to bring godly standards and virtue to these industries. Esther competed and got selected in a pageant for beautiful young virgins. The journey to fulfil God's purpose for one's life may take several routes.

EXCHANGE AT THE GATES: UP TO HALF THE KINGDOM

Gate serves as a place of entry and exit; a door between one side of a fence and the other.

I use the term to symbolise transition into a next phase, dimension or manifestation.

The devil took Jesus to a very high mountain, and showed him all the kingdoms of the world and their splendour. All Jesus had to do was to bow down and worship, "all this I will give you" he said to Him. Jesus was given an offer of kingdoms of the world, Esther was offered up-to-half the kingdom.

❖ ❖ ❖

Whenever there is an opportunity to accomplish divine agenda, there can be those moments where one's true motive is tested. Am I in this for me or Him? In ministry we must come to that place where when the Employer(The Lord) asks us to lay our tools down, we lay it down. When He asks us to pick it up, we pick it up.

There has been plane crashes, motor accidents and untimely deaths because people wanted to be in the meeting more than the Convener of the meeting. When we ran an errand for the Lord, we must subject ourselves to His superintendence and administration. He is not only a saviour, he is our Lord.

People pleasing and quest for validation has caused many to lose their place and plot in divine script.

There were occasions people wanted to seize Jesus and make him King because of the many miracles and wonders He performed, but he would always discern and walk away. The cross comes before the Kingship and Jesus understood this.

In each of the eight requests Esther made to the King, she was presented with the blank cheque of up-to-half the kingdom. This is that place where many have missed it and exchanged their heritage- inheritance, for bread and lentil stew. (as happened in the case of Esau and Jacob)

Esther was ready to sacrifice her throne, in order that divine will would prevail. But in so doing, she saved her throne, her own life and that of her people. She was steadfast, purposeful and grounded in all situations and at all times.

Further reading: (Matt 4:8-9, Gen 25:34)

HOW EXCHANGE OCCUR AT THE GATES

Weariness

There are those times when one is weary. Life situations can make one weary, family situations can cause weariness, loneliness can cause weariness.

At the time of Haman's plot, Esther was going through her own time of emotional turmoil and feeling of abandonment.

She relays how the King had not invited her for the past thirty days. The way she put it tells how distressed she might have been feeling about the situation. Esth 4:11

It was like she was saying I myself, I am not finding my feet. I thought I was the Queen. I thought I was the most lovely, the most beautiful. How come all these concubines are being invited by the King and I am not. In these early stages of her marriage, the honeymoon is not going according to plan.

Feeling of weariness can so much cloud one's judgement and actions. Thus, it is really vital we build a system of support around us. A loving and welcoming home, a good social circle of friends and family one can reach out to.

It was a weary Esau, that took stew and despised his birth right.

Materialism

Materialism is a false belief that riches, possessions and luxury are the most important things in life.

Judas Iscariot sold his Jesus and place among the twelve for 30 pieces of silver.

(In Hebrew culture, thirty pieces of silver was the exact price paid to the master of a slave if his slave was killed accidentally whiles working for someone. example, if they were gored by an ox)

Possessions may get one a house but not a home. It may get one a bed but not rest. It may buy medication but not health. Such things as love, joy, peace which are invaluable are not measured by material possession.

Further reading:(Matt 26:15, Exodus 21:32)

Time Such As This

Epoch refers to an era, window or a particular time/ place in history.

Much of human life revolve around time. Mordecai said to Esther, who knows if you have come to the kingdom for such a time as this.

Certain people exchanged their divine estate because they could not discern the time. Daniel understood that after 70 years, desolation of Jerusalem should end. There was a 400-year time span for the children of Israel to complete servitude. There are time sensitive commissions and one's inability to discern the times could lead to an exchange. Mordecai in essence said to Esther, deliverance would surely happen. When you miss it, it will arise from another place but you would forego an opportunity to write your name and that of your family's in gold.

It is in my best interest to seize the moment. I do not outrun the pacesetter, and I do not lag. I keep in harmony, union, in tune with the Conductor.

Further reading: (Dan 9:2, Gen 15:13)

Love Of The Apparel

Esther was ready to lay down her royalty and crown. Please picture the six months of myrrh treatments. Picture another six of beauty preparations and all the effort that goes into attaining that status, coming from the humble background of an orphan. Yet Esther was willing to lay down the apparel. Ungodly exchange has happened because some got accustomed to the pump and pageantry associated with the costume. They forget those positions were vehicles, not destinations.

Should we love the gifts more than the Giver of gifts? It is a misplaced priority to go after the gift, instead of the Giver of gifts, the Source. It is not in the numbers, certifications, accolades, Angels at our disposal etc. Stay connected to the Source.

Routine

Esther was ready to evolve. When she presented herself to be Queen, she might have envisioned comfort, pleasure, prominence. What Mordecai was presenting may not have been in her own scripts. When we get accustomed to routine, evolving becomes a nightmare.

Esther knew when to evolve from ceremonials to purpose.

Through her act of wise service, many people of other nationalities decided to become Jews (Esth 8: 17).

The evangelists, revivalists and apostles are not those who carry megaphones and microphones, not all heroes wear capes.

Aversion To Change

King David had slayed giants, groomed able lieutenants and raised a formidable army. This time in 2 Sam 21:17 he was nearly killed at a battle for he grew faint. His team said to him, "You shall go out no more with us to battle, lest you quench the lamp of Israel".

David evolved and took his place as a luminary, giving wise counsel and direction and gathering cedar, gold and other materials for the building of a temple for the Lord.

There is nothing to prove, validation comes from above. There is a time to evolve.

ESTHER QUALITIES

Discipline

Discipline is the ability to see through a project and adapt at all its different stages. It is the competence to run with order.

Esther run a multifaceted, dynamic and integrated scheme involving herself, King Ahasuerus, the Jewish people, Mordecai, her team and staff. Incredible how she executed the script so correctly each time.

Secure

Esther was secure in herself and abilities. She recognised what she had the capacity to do and what others should be entrusted with. She trusted the wisdom, counsel and intellect of Mordecai. It is said of Ahithophel that the advice which he gave, was as though one had enquired at the oracle of God. (2 Sam 16:23).

Been secure is acknowledging our strengths and also the strength and gifts in others. When Jesus prayed in Gethsemane, an Angel came to strengthen him, also a human-Simon the Cyrene who helped him carry the cross to Golgotha.

May we not disdain the helpers, who come our way. It is our cross, but some people may be sent to make the journey more bearable.

Discernment

Esther's ability to discern the times is one of her most outstanding attributes.

Certain people have such abilities, for example it is said of the children of Issachar that, they had understanding of the times and what Israel ought to do at every step.

At the first banquet granted by the King, Esther made no mention of Haman's plot. When the King could not sleep one night and honoured Mordecai, Esther discerned that a divine hand was at work, now was the time. The following banquet, she made her request and it was granted. She could perceive when the time was right, gleaning confirmation from unfolding events.

Esther's request for prayer or supernatural backing, was also an admission that it was a hard task to accomplish in the natural.

She Knew Her Place

She understood though she was the queen, access to the King was not a given and that it was the King's prerogative.

There are protocols and systems that govern thrones, human and all spiritual endeavour. Esther was well versed in palace protocol and regulation. She was cognisant of the rules and also their exceptions. There are consequences for breaches.

There are so many lessons to glean from Esther and her approach to things.

TEAM WORK: THE ROLE OF MORDECAI

Mordecai is the typical marketplace Apostle. The Apostles of the marketplace normally operate a combination of the seven spirits of the Lord -knowledge, understanding, wisdom, counsel, might, lordship and fear of the Lord.

Mordecai would not pay homage to Haman. These Apostles are not afraid to stand up for what is right. They are fathers, this would show in how he brought up Esther, also his great concern for her. It is said that each day, he paced in front of the quarters to learn of Esther's welfare and how she was doing.

Mordecai worked so seamlessly with Esther, through team work to bring about deliverance for his people.

Further reading: (Is 11:2, Rev 3:1, Rev 4:5)

Information

Mordecai had his ear on the ground. There is the "palace bubble". Certain high level positions detach one from the realities on the ground, the plight of the everyday person. That is why it is important for the Esthers' to have a Mordecai who is well grounded. Mordecai was the person who relayed the plot to kill the King. He was diligent and painstaking.

Denominationalism

Esther and Mordecai worked together to achieve a common goal.

The Apostles, Prophets, Evangelists etc. are a gift to edify the body of Christ. They are not given to a congregation, an assembly or a denomination. Sometimes it might be necessary to leverage on the unique gifts of a person elsewhere, been it healing, teaching or intercession. It is rare to find a Prophet or Apostle raised solely from a single denomination. They might start out as Catholics, journey through some Charismatic churches and end up in a Pentecostal church. They glean from all these places; they are made by the body for the body!

> The prophecy of Joel is that in those days He will pour out His spirit on all flesh.

> I am not the only one that God poured His spirit on. I receive and draw from others.

Further reading: (Eph 4:11, Joel 2:28,29)

Institutionalised The Feast Of Purim

Mordecai institutionalised the celebration of this feast for his people, to be marked on the fourteenth day of the month of Adar.

Apostles build people and systems. With the grace of Apostleship, Jethro counselled Moses to set up systems, in order that he might preserve himself. Jesus did not put up a church building, he built people. The change we want to see in society starts with people. Build your children, your home, this overflows to communities and nations.

Knowledgeable

Mordecai was the one who came up with counter legislation to empower his people to defend themselves, working with the King's scribes. He also wrote instructions and sent letters to the Jews in all the provinces. He was astute and knowledgeable.

While the author of the book of Esther is unknown, it is thought to have been written by either Mordecai or Ezra. Mordecai is such an important figure in Jewish history.

Truth

The belt of truth is an important armour of God. Sometimes healing would only come by swallowing bitter pills.

Mordecai exhibits honesty, integrity and understanding of

divinity. He tells Esther the truth rather than massage her ego.

Mordecai understands that the plan of God override evil, that deliverance would surely happen. If Esther would not rise to the occasion, salvation would come from another place.

It is a bit simple so to speak, to assume I am the only person on God's program. There are so many people placed strategically, to execute the divine masterplan. There are 7000 in Israel who have not bowed to Baal. It is therefore an honour to play a part in divine plot.

Further reading: (1 Kgs 19:18, Eph 6:10-20)

CHAPTER 8

JOSEPH

Joseph is one of twelve sons of Jacob and the eldest of two sons born to Rachel. Gideon, who I discussed in chapter 3, was of the tribe of Joseph(Manasseh). Joseph received the double portion of inheritance. His two sons were adopted as sons by Jacob, thereby obtaining one portion above his brothers. Joseph's sons, Ephraim and Manasseh- would become the dominant tribe in the north of Israel, Judah the dominant in the south.

Jacob loved Joseph more than all his other children and made him a tunic of many colours. While he was a child, Joseph had visions of his future in the form of dreams and he would share them with his brothers and father. These visions of greatness invited envy and loathing.

The brothers plotted to kill Joseph by their own hand. That plan changed on account of Reuben proffering otherwise. Another brother, Judah then suggested they sell him instead. Joseph was sold to Ishmaelite traders as a slave for 20 shekels of silver. The Ishmaelites took him to Egypt where he ends up in the household of Potiphar, an officer of Pharaoh and captain of the palace regiment. Several turn of events and divine orchestrations would see Joseph assume a position of governor in Egypt. The story of Joseph explains the residence of Israel in Egypt.

Further reading: (Gen chapters 30-50, Ezk 47:13, Ps 100:17-25)

JOSEPH'S CALL TO THE MARKETPLACE

Joseph was a governor in Egypt. He excelled in that role and saved the nation from what would be the effect of seven years of drought and severe famine. He was an administrator extraordinaire. In Potiphar's house he had charge of the household; overseer of the house and all in the field. In the dungeon, he helped manage his fellow prisoners.

There are those who are called to the area of administration, management and governance. They are placed in these places to preserve lives and crack tough cases and challenges, using godly wisdom and virtue. Joseph became a father to the Pharaoh. (a high ranking advisor, to Pharaoh)

I AM JOSEPH

Joseph made this statement twice, on the occasion he chose to reveal his identity to his brothers in Egypt.

> The brothers seized Joseph's tunic and put him in a pit.

> But Joseph's greatness was not in his coat of many colours.

Potiphar's wife also took Joseph's cloth while Joseph run, to escape sin.

You may take my clothes. What I need is me. If I have me, I will have my clothes back.

> *Joseph did not remain uncovered forever. He fulfilled his dreams, he was adorned in royal regalia and clothed in garments of fine linen.*

Affirmations and confessions are a great way to enhance one's self-esteem. Positive confession is the physical/ vocal expression and agreement with the good promises about one's life stored in the heavenly places.

Further reading: (Eph 1:3-6)

I AM JOSEPH, 7-DAYS OF POSITIVE CONFESSION

I am Joseph, I am a fruitful bough. I have an overflowing anointing.

I am blessed with the dew of the heaven above. I am blessed with the fat of the earth.

I am the salt of the earth; I carry the flavour of God, I season the earth.

I am a royal prince/princess in my generation. I have been set apart, consecrated for such a time as this. I am a voice and a gift to my generation. My voice is heard on the mountains. I am unleashed to roar. I have a message to share and a story to tell. I am someone to be listened to.

My steps are ordered; my feet carry the gospel of peace. I am a bearer of good tidings.

I am alive for such a time as this. I bring light into darkness. I am a lighthouse!

I thrive and prosper in the things I do. I am blessed and I am a blessing. I am loved. I am loving. I am lovely.

My hands are blessed; I carry the favour and goodwill of God to everything I touch.

Because my hands have been made strong, by the hands of the Almighty. The Mighty God of Israel.

Further reading: (Gen 49:22, Deut 33:13-16)

I AM JOSEPH: 14-DAYS OF POSITIVE CONFESSION

I am Joseph, I have an excellent spirit. I carry the essence of the seven spirits of God.

Seven is for perfection, I carry the sevenfold spirit of God. I have within me the perfect spirit- the Holy Spirt, with the evidence of speaking in tongues.

I carry the spirit of wisdom. My wisdom is from above; it comes from heaven. My wisdom is righteous and peace-loving. it is considerate, it is impartial and sincere. My wisdom is full of mercy and good fruit. The fear of the Lord is the beginning of my wisdom.

I overflow with the fear of the Lord.

I have the spirit of knowledge within me. I learn, unlearn and relearn. I am malleable.

I have understanding. I discern the times; I know what ought to be done in each season. The knowledge of the Holy One is understanding.

I carry the spirit of Lordship. I am a leader, I lead my myself first, then others. I overflow with good counsel. I take counsel and I give counsel.

I stand up for truth, I stand up for justice, I stand up for righteousness. The stone the builders did not accept has now become the chief cornerstone.

I am a mighty warrior in the name of Jesus!

Further reading: (Jam 3:13, Rev 5:6, Is 11:2, Prov 9:10)

JOSEPH'S DREAMS

Judah, Levi and the brothers didn't know that there was no need to fight Joseph. They were carrying equal measure of greatness - Kings, Priests, Judges. Everyone is blessed, they were all stars.

Joseph's dream was God's dream. It was a path set several years beforehand when He made a covenant with Abraham. He said to him, "know for certain" that your descendants shall end up in a foreign land for four hundred years. In other words, it was like surely this shall happen, there would be an incubation period in Egypt. Joseph was simply set apart, consecrated to play a part in divine script.

The Plumb Line

Our spiritual walk can be likened to a karaoke performance, or a musician playing to a backing track or metronome. You keep in step with the tempo or you go off-beat. God is our metronome; he is our tempo. We don't sing however we feel to sing, in whatever way. When God said to Abraham, walk before Me and be blameless, it meant to keep in step and at pace with Him-I AM the pacemaker, the plumb line.

The End Or The Means?

If it is a God dream then let it happen by righteousness, for He leads us on a path of righteousness for His name sake. Joseph was not going to cut corners. In Potiphar's house when faced with temptation, Joseph would not sin against God. He would not be ungrateful or wicked towards Potiphar his master.

In pursuing dreams that we believe has been put in our hearts by God, the process towards attaining it sometimes would count more than achieving those dreams.

In secular or commercial settings, there is this mantra "the End justifies the means". In God, the means is equally as important.

Jesus had to suffer death by crucifixion, He had to be wounded for our transgression. He had to be bruised for our iniquities, and we are healed by his stripes. And because not one of his bones should be broken, the soldiers would not break the Messiah's legs on the cross. The means matter, in God.

> When the children of Israel thirst in the desert, Moses was asked to speak to the rock. Moses struck the rock twice. There was results, water gushed; the people drank. However, the Lord was not pleased and so Moses would not take the children of Israel to the promised land, only his eyes would see. The means matter.

In God, obedience is better than sacrifice. Saul the King lost his royal estate in similar fashion. Saul offered a sacrifice that was for Samuel to offer.

At another time, he failed yet again to heed to divine directions. He took plunder of sheep, oxen and choice things. Actually he purposed to sacrifice them for the Lord. God was not looking for sacrifices at that time.

What seemed to have worked one moment, may not be what is required another time. It is about obedience and righteousness. It is not about zeal; we do the Master's bidding. He is our plumbline.

Totally Yielded

Mostly, God would test you with your Isaac. That Isaac would be that same promise you have trained many years for. The same thing you have prayed for many years about. You must reach the point where you are willing to lay down your Isaac on the altar. When God can trust you at that point,

then blessings He will bless you, multiplying He will multiply you. Your descendants shall be stars and numerous. You shall have a lasting legacy.

<u>But even if,</u>

This brazen phrase came about because Shadrach, Meshach and

Abednego would not bow to King Nebuchadnezzar's idol. They were going to face the fiery inferno. They knew God was able to deliver them but then they added, even if that does not happen they would not serve a false god.

We are not in this faith because of what we would like to be blessed with. It is not because of material wealth. It is not to prove a point or to make a case. Neither is it to satisfy our ego.

Muslims drive good cars, pagans buy mansions, atheist own thriving businesses. There are lots of millionaires in China, a country with a vast population who are mostly non-religious or practice Buddhism and Taoism.

If all our hope in Christ is for this life alone, then we are to be the most pitied among all people.

Further reading: (Is 53:5, Jn 19:36, Num 20:7-11, 1 Sam 13:13, 1 Sam 15:22, Ps 23:3, Gen 17:1, Gen 22:17-19, Dan 3:12-30, 1 Corin 15:19)

STAR HUNTERS

I find it troubling, that Joseph's brothers were actually going to kill Joseph by themselves. They planned to kill him and then bury his body in a pit. When I imagine, how they were going to do that, it makes me understand that people can be really callous. It was Reuben who suggested that instead of killing him with their own hands, Joseph be left in a pit to die by himself. (he planned to rescue him thereafter).

Jesus told us to not fear those who can kill the body. We should rather fear Him who can destroy both soul and body in hell. I use this text to make a point. With care, caution and precaution one may be able to protect themselves from physical harm. What If those who plan to harm you deploy spiritual methods. How do you protect yourself from those who attack your soul and destiny?

Joseph's brothers said, "we shall see what will become of his dreams!" People may attack you physically because of your dreams, star, destiny, purpose. Others too attack your soul and spirit on account of your dreams.

The Woman, The Child And The Dragon

In Rev 12:4, a dragon stood before a woman who was ready to give birth, to devour the child as soon as it was born.

This episode is what sometimes befall people of great destiny. The dragon's appetite for the child is because of his destiny (a ruler of the nations).

When someone is poised or elected as a candidate to be President or to take up an important public service, newspapers begin to dig into the person's past. They dig their social media posts, past associations, even to when they were in primary school. All sort of revelations begin to come up. Often times this is the handiwork of competitors and opponents, though sometime too it is a reflection of people's appetite to know more about their new President or Minister.

It is so also when someone has a call to an office in the body of Christ. (Apostle, Prophet, Pastor etc) The same when they are to play a role in divine scheme or they find themself on divine calendar.

Once the person is born, he/she generate interest. Evil says, "we will see what would become of those dreams!". This explains the hostility on your life and why you face such unprecedented attacks.

People sometimes ask, what have I done to deserve this? The answer is, it is because of your star, your influence, the impact you will make on other people's lives.

Your assignment to your own family; to change it for the better. That determination to break besetting patterns of single parenting, alcoholism, sickness, abortions, poverty. What you have come into this world to add to the quality of life and your positive influence on your generation.

Wise Men See Baby Jesus' Star/Destiny

Wise men from the East, saw the star of Jesus and came to worship. For these men to make that journey, means they were 100% certain about their metaphysical and astrological art. At that time there were no cars. They rode on camels for miles. They also carried gifts, they were that sure.

At Philippi, the leading city in the district of Macedonia a lady described as a fortune teller followed after Paul, Silas and their team saying, "these men are servants of the Most High God, who proclaim to you the way of salvation". And that was right, she so accurately identified who they were.

The source is the distinction, otherwise the spirit realm is an open space.

IMPORTANCE OF PROPHETS

All other faiths have those who can access the spirit realm. Prophets play that role in the Christian faith. The gift of prophecy is not the same as the office of the Prophet. It starts with gift of prophecy and graduate to the office. The Prophetic, is a field of practice.

In the health service we have a doctor who is a general practitioner. We also have those who have specialised in certain fields like skin, women health, child health, heart, surgery etc.

Prophets attain the office after several years of spiritual training. There are those prophets who specialise in the past, others in the present and others, the future.

They have the capacity to see manipulation and hindrances and the ability to ward off evil hands in order to bring solution and restoration to a matter. Prophets would be able to tell if one's star is under manipulation by evil hands.

> Prophesying is the seeing, hearing and speaking bit; bringing solution through counsel and spiritual action make up the restoration bit.

The eye is an important organ in the body. Apostle Paul admonished that we do not despise prophecy and for that matter Prophets.

I believe the killing of the kid goat by the brothers and dipping Joseph's robe in the blood was a prophetic act. This was a spiritual action they performed on Joseph's behalf, unbeknown to them. From that time onwards, the blood would speak for Joseph. He began overcoming the pitfalls, entrapments, isolation. We overcome by the blood of the lamb and by the word of our testimony.

When our spiritual gifts work together with physical discipline and has the backing of the foundation of Jesus' blood then all doors will open. We shall see the manifestation of those dreams, in Jesus name!

Further reading: (1 Thes 5:20, Matt 10:28, Rev 12:1-6, Rev 12:11, Matt 2:1-2, Acts 16:17, 1 Corin 12:12-27)

LESSONS FROM JOSEPH

Delivery Of Prophecy

The third commandment sets out that we do not mention the name of the Lord in vain. Anyone who does that will not be exonerated. Three is an important number in the Christian faith, so this commandment is not to be taken lightly.

In most Jewish tests, the word God is not written in full. It is instead written as G_d. Even in this book I have tried as much as possible to make use of words like divine, supernatural, Lord, Angel etc. to avoid the superfluous use of God. The name of the

Lord is reverent.

Joseph would say, I had this dream. It is a sign of spiritual immaturity when people would indiscriminately use phrases like, God told me this, God showed me this dream.

Pharaoh the Egyptian King (an idol worshipper) had a dream that 100% manifested. The spirit realm is an open space.

When there is a vision, dream, word in your spirit, in your ears etc., it is best to describe it as such, making distinctions where necessary. When Mary was to bear Jesus, it was an Angel that appeared to her.

Mary did not go to Elizabeth saying, God told me I will give birth to God. No one has seen the Father except the Son, for no one can see God and live.

Further reading: (Exodus 20:7, Deut 5:11, Jn 6:46, Jn 1:18, Exodus 33:20)

Patience

There are certain things that would only happen by a set time. For example, it takes approximately nine months for a baby to be conceived and delivered. A degree takes 3-4 years to be completed etc. So it is with our faith walk. It is possible to get to a place where things must take their natural course. Joseph endured, persevered and suffered long (long suffering) but eventually, he did get out of the pit. He got out of Potiphar's house and he got out of the shackles of prison into the palace. Let us imitate those who through faith and patience inherit the promises.

Further reading: (Heb 6:12)

Good Character

The foundation and pillar of Christianity is character. In pursuit of our dreams and aspirations we must minimise the feet we step on, the people we hurt, the homes we wreck.

The bread knife forgets the bread; the bread remembers.

Joseph would not sin against God or show wickedness towards Potiphar by breaking his home. God is love and love is patient. Love is kind, it does not envy, it does not dishonour others. Love is not self-seeking.

Further reading: (1 Corin 13)

CHAPTER 9

NEHEMIAH

Nehemiah served in the court of King Artaxerxes in Persia. He was the King's cupbearer (an advisor with responsibility of keeping the King from been poisoned with a drink). He held the king's cup, meanwhile he was despondent about the condition of the walls of Jerusalem. He lived in Persia but his heart was in Jerusalem. His people are left vulnerable in the absence of a wall. They face reproach and mockery from their enemies.

The story begins in the book of Ezra and is completed in Nehemiah. The Hebrew Bible recognise Ezra and Nehemiah as a single book.

Following more than 60 years in Babylonian captivity, King Cyrus of Persia issues an edict that willing Jews may return to Jerusalem to rebuild the temple and the City.

The first returnees were under the supervision of Zerubbabel. The first group managed to complete the reconstruction of the temple. They faced discouragement from the non-Jewish inhabitants and even ceased the construction at one point.

The second group under the guidance of Ezra, came during the reign of Persian King Artaxerxes, nearly 60 years after the first batch. During this time there was a spiritual reformation. Ezra led the people to repentance, consecration and temple worship was enhanced.

Then Nehemiah arrives as governor of Judaea. He uses his political influence to support Ezra; he brought hope and restoration to the people. The walls of the city were rebuilt in a record 52 days.

This was done, not without obstacles. There was discouragement, mockery, threats and conspiracies but Nehemiah led the people with vision, grit, wisdom and compassion to complete the project.

NEHEMIAH'S CALL TO THE MARKETPLACE

Nehemiah felt called to the area of public service, assuming the position of governor of Judaea. He was granted this office after much prayer, supplication and intercession.(chapter 1) His concern for his people was rooted in prayer, therefore he saw the King's willingness to send him to Jerusalem as an answer from God. He would often mention, "what God had put in my heart to do at Jerusalem".

There are people like Nehemiah who would be called to the area of public service. They would be governors of schools, serve in the councils, serve as mayors and as governors of state.

They are strategically placed or sent as answer to prayer. They will bring hope, offer protection, increase comfort and carry relief to people.

When certain nobles and community leaders were overburdening the masses with taxes and dues in what Nehemiah saw as usury, he called on them to cease. He himself refrained from asking for food portions, which he was entitled to as governor from the people. Nehemiah had compassion and brought righteousness and justice to that office.

A CALL TO AMBIDEXTERITY

There is this pattern I have observed from Gideon, Esther, Nehemiah and all the others. There seems to be this divine desire that, for "such a time as this" God's people should not be comfortable keeping divinity in their rooms and in tabernacles. There is a nudge for an outpouring into homes and into the world. A people who would build and rebuild with one hand while with the other, they watch with drawn swords. This two-edged approach is what I term, a call to ambidexterity. We are not to lose sight of the frontline; the schools, the prisons, the hospitals, technology, music while we go about engaging the ethereal.

◆ ◆ ◆

Up on the high mountain of transfiguration, Peter would say, Lord it is good and wonderful for us to be here. Let us build a tabernacle one for you, one for Moses and one for Elijah. They were so much enjoying the serenity of divinity and the supernatural; there was a cloud of glory and open heavens. But Jesus would say to Peter, James and John arise!

Peter's words echo what often is the case with faith~ the supernatural could offer a peace, aura and ambience that is abiding even absorbing.

We are not to inhale and not exhale. We breath in and breath out. There is an outflowing. Let us arise, shine, for our light has come and the glory of the Lord has risen upon us.

Further reading: (Matt 17:4, Is 60:1)

APOSTOLIC DISPENSATION

It seems to me that the pandemic ushered the body of Christ into another dispensation, the Apostolic dispensation. Apostle comes from the Greek root, *apostolos* meaning "one who is sent out". In this epoch, members of the body are being sent out as ambassadors, envoys and voice of God to the area of commerce, education, law & order, governance and enterprise. A people who will carry godly virtue to the community, society, the nations and to the ends of the world. Whether called to altar ministry, pulpit ministry or marketplace ministry; we must not lose sight of what is happening in the world around us. We must repurpose, reprogram and reorient to herald the coming of His kingdom among us. His kingdom, come!

Further reading: (*Pray to discover your place and role in this dispensation*)

REVIVAL ARCHITECTURE

All revivals have these five appendages or arms.

Evangelistic Arm.

This happens when The Holy Spirit would cause a spark in people's hearts and they begin to travel all over and into all spaces, spreading the message of the good news of Christ, often as missionaries and evangelists.

Pastoral Arm

After the evangelists and missionaries bring the good news, there is normally the need for those who believe to be gathered and discipled. So a generation of Pastors are raised; to gather. The harvest is already there, it is a matter now of gathering and pastoring.

Teaching Arm

Great teachers arise to divide the word of truth and to teach. They would espouse holiness, righteous living, neighbourliness and fundamental christian doctrine.

Prophetic Arm

Church at a point become a religious routine and the gift of the Holy Spirit is relegated to the background. So another dispensation come to stir up the gifts; healing gifts, prophetic gifts etc.

The Apostolic Dispensation

The church is being sent out, to be a lighthouse. A people who would bring light to a dark world.

The purpose of this book Mine Lighthouse, is to announce this dispensation and help one person find their location, role and place in revival architecture.

> The difference between evangelists sent out and apostles is this: Apostles carry an anointing of Lordship that evangelists do not have. They come with governing authority, understanding and insight. Apostles are the elite unit in kingdom army, the Navy Seals.

STRATEGY FOR APOSTOLIC DISPENSATION

The marketplace is not an oasis. It is a continuum, an extension of divine infrastructure. Whereas mainstream church would lead revivals, transformation and renewal, revival is normally ushered by intercessors, sisters and nuns, prophets and people in secret places, on prayer mountains etc.

ALTAR IS BUILT AND SACRIFICES BEGIN (ALTAR MINISTRY)

Under the auspices of Zerubbabel, the returnees rebuild the altar and begin to offer sacrifices and burnt offerings to the Lord.

This stage deals with issues of covenants, territorial and spiritual legalities. For example, it was a supernatural encounter Abraham had that beget the 400-years captivity in Egypt. To break out of that slavery time schedule, that covenant package has to be renegotiated on the altar. So for example, If I was a Hebrew slave living in Egypt and I got angry it would not solve the problem. If I attempted to escape it would not succeed. An insurrection would fail.

◆ ◆ ◆

Moses killing the Egyptian in the fight involving the Hebrew did not bring a solution, it actually made matters worse for him.

The root cause has to be tackled as priority. God would normally deal with the root cause of issues, as happened with sin-He sent Jesus to die. Moses eventually had to go to Jethro to study covenant protocols and altar practice.

For the most part, Israel's captivity was the result of breaking covenant between them and the Lord by serving other gods; disobedience and spiritual infidelity.

Further reading: (Gen 15:13, Exodus 2:11-12, Jer 25:11-12, Dan 9:3-19, 1 Sam 1:11)

TEMPLE RECONSTRUCTION (PULPIT MINISTRY)

The temple is reconstructed and completed under Zerubbabel. Ezra leads another group of exiles back and begins to teach proper temple worship and lead the people into spiritual reformation and renewal.

Mainstream church is the training ground for people to discover their role and location in God's kingdom agenda. Right worship and unity of the body is key, if church is to serve that purpose of being a fertile breeding and training ground for God's children.

Unity Among The Body

One body different parts: Nehemiah engaged the co-operation of all the people to complete the walls, each household or group raised a specific segment brick by brick. This unity of purpose is what the church is called into.

When water is mixed with oil they are united, but the oil is at the top, water is at the bottom. That is not the kind of unity. This unity is that achieved when salt or sugar is mixed with water, a homogenous solution where both are totally united in purpose and solidarity.

> *In a football team (comparing to the body of Christ), there is a goalkeeper, there are defenders, there are midfielders, there is a striker. Together, they make the team. Now even among the defenders, there are lateral defenders and central defenders.*

We all cannot be goalkeepers; we won't have a team then. The team cannot field eleven strikers, that will not work either.

It is good that people know, they are not all encompassing.

They are part of a network, a team, a body; some Apostles, some Prophets, some Evangelists, Teachers, Pastors etc. It is OK for different congregations and denominations to emphasise certain doctrine or specific aspects of the gospel. It is in accordance with their ability and purpose.

Right Worship

Jesus went into the temple on one occasion where He overturned tables of the money changers and the seats of those who sold doves; my house shall be called a house of prayer, he said.

Now Jesus continued and said, tear down this temple and I will raise it again in three days; the temple he had spoken of was his body.

Likewise, if our body is likened to the Lord's temple, then it must be cleared of all unrighteous inhabitants. The topic of cohabiting of The Holy Spirit and familial spirit is broad and out of the scope of this book. However, I want to make the point that there is such a thing as consecration/sanctification. Ungodly covenants must be broken to give Christ sole proprietorship of our whole being; spirit, body and soul.

When people are conflicted by two voices in their hearts and within, it is an indication of cohabitation.

❖ ❖ ❖

The parable of Jesus about wheat and tares will help you understand what is going on. Good seed is sown, but along the way some previous generation or even ourselves entangle our lives with other spirits by going to palm readers, fortune tellers, shrines etc. That is how access is gained into our lives.

When we come into Christ, the goal is to reach a place of maturity(Prophet/Apostle stage). This is that stage, we begin to remove these tares that stifle our growth and potential.

> The reason for the gift of discernment of spirits is to ascertain from which fountain a person is ministering from.

One must make way for the other. Deliverance Prophets are gifted with the knowledge to close channels in our souls and break one free from those covenants that grant such access unto our human spirit. This is how we manifest our divine destinies. Selah

Further reading: (1 Corin 12:12-27, Luke 19:11-13, Matt 21:12-13, 1 Thes 5:23, Jn 2:19-22, Eph 4:11-16, Matt 13:24-30)

CITY WALLS RECONSTRUCTED (THE MARKETPLACE)

Nehemiah comes to rebuild the walls of Jerusalem. According to James, faith without works is dead. This is where we show our faith by deed and action and not by mere words. The call to the marketplace is the call to show our faith by our works.

This is that place where we see His Kingdom in action and in deed; be it in our homes or kind acts of service, holy legislation, financing or the promotion of just causes.

Here we have the marketplace Apostles like Nehemiah and Mordecai serving in places of authority, Prophets like Daniel who offer counsel & direction, Teachers like Nicodemus, Pastors like Naomi and Evangelists like Esther.

> The grounds are cleared at the altar, the people are primed from the pulpit and when the time is right, the called to the marketplace spring into action.

These choice servants of our Lord have been placed strategically in positions and places to bring help in times of need and to govern righteously.

His kingdom come, His will be done on earth.

Further reading: (Jam 2:14-18, Matt 7:24-27)

OPPOSITION TO ONE'S CALL

When a commission is divine, it does not necessarily mean there will not be obstacles in achieving them. There may be times of frustration, even plots and schemes to thwart that project but we would learn from Nehemiah that it is possible to overcome and build.

Opposition From Without

At certain times external forces would be that opposition. This may involve unfair legislation, a hostile environment or opposition in the form of doubters and mockers. Nehemiah faced mockery, threats and indignation from individuals such as Sanballat, Tobiah and Geshem. He also met resistance from communities; the Arabs, the Ammonites and the Ashdodites.

We could learn resilience, determination, wisdom and focus from Nehemiah, who remained steadfast, tenacious, devoted and committed to his commission.

Opposition From Within

There was Shemaiah the prophet who was hired to dissuade and distract Nehemiah in his rebuilding of the walls.

It was Nehemiah's high level of discernment that thwarted this treachery. Jesus was tempted with scripture. He was tempted saying, it is written that the angels would take charge over you. Would you jump then, if you are the Son of God? There is no point to prove, validation is from above.

The story of the Young Prophet and the Old prophet, which I briefly share in chapter 10 teach that the area of our vulnerability would be from those we call buddies, family, kindred, from within. The young Prophet would not go to Jeroboam the King's house to dine. However, when another prophet approached, he budged, lost the plot and met untimely death.

We must come to a place of maturity, spiritual knowledge and understanding in our faith walk to be able to discern between urgency and emergency. To tell between what is above and what is from above.

Further reading: (Matt 4:1-11, 1Kgs 13)

CHAPTER 10

EPISTERIZO

According to Thayer's Greek lexicon, episterizo means to render more firm or to strengthen more. In this chapter I share foundational realities in Christianity, ancient truths that would bolster your faith infrastructure.

DO NOT WORRY

"Therefore I say to you, do not worry about your life, what you will eat or what you will drink; nor about your body, what you will put on ... Your heavenly Father knows that you need these things. **But seek first the kingdom of God and His righteousness, and all these things shall be added to you.**

Therefore do not worry about tomorrow, your future is in His hands, the One who holds tomorrow.

Interconnectedness

The link between not worrying and getting provision lies in the understanding of God's kingdom and decrypting of His righteousness. Peace is available. There can be wealth in the midst of scarcity, health challenges can be resolved, tragedies and unwholesome family patterns can be settled. The code is in cracking kingdom principles.

It is crucial one is grounded on foundations of truth and not presumptions, when it comes to faith. The lowest level of knowledge is assumption.

"Keep back your servant also from **presumptuous sins**"Let them not hold sway over me. David said this in his songs in the book of psalms.

Our God is the ancient of days. We have not received the gracious calling into His kingdom to come and change Him- He is the unchangeable God. We have been called to seek, understand and walk before him (be guided, guarded and gourd by Him). He is God Almighty, El Shaddai.

Understanding kingdom principles provide the sturdy structure required for a steady growth in the faith.

Further reading: (Matt 6: 25-34, Ps 19:13, Gen 17:1)

FULL GOSPEL

To different members of the body, has He committed unique ability and revelation. It is the aggregation or sum total, that produce the full gospel. No one is all encompassing. Revelation is progressive. Apostle Paul said, when I was a child I spoke as a child, I understood as a child, I thought as a child. But when he became an adult, he put away childish things.

One can be correct about salvation and forgiveness but incomplete about other matters. Another may be right about various topics such as loyalty, church administration and prayer, but growing when it comes to knowledge of salvation and God's forgiveness. Discern therefore what to humbly learn from and what to humbly unlearn in a Minister's teaching. Till we all come to the unity of the faith, to the measure of the stature of the fullness of Christ.

Further reading: (Eph 4:13, 1 Corin 13:11)

3-TYPES OF CALL BASED ON ENCOUNTER

When Jesus said go and make disciples of all nations; baptise them in the name of the Father, of the Son and of the Holy Spirit (Matt 28:19-20), that baptism was not the liturgical construct or the sign of the cross or even baptism of water. Scripture acknowledges several kinds of baptism. There is baptism of water, baptism into Christ(Rom 6:3, Gal 3:27), the Holy Ghost baptism, the baptism of fire and even baptism for the dead.
This baptism means to introduce, initiate or immerse these disciples into the knowledge, ways, domain of the Godhead. (the Father, the Son and the Holy Spirit)

On the basis of this charge, there are people who are called to teach and demonstrate the workings of the Holy Spirit. Others are also well versed in matters of the Son, while some have very deep understanding of the Father. The duty of the believer is to have the full experience of the Godhead.

Further reading: (Heb 6:1-3)

The Call Of The Father

Those who have the call of the Father tend to have good command and understanding of the laws that govern humans and nature and the ways of the Creator. (The Father is the creator of the heavens and the earth). Joshua could command the Sun to stand still. Jesus used the soil(nature) to heal a blind man. (John 5:4). These Ministers may pray over water (during the time of Jesus, an Angel would come and stir the pool and anyone who stepped in the water first was healed), anointing oils etc and use these for healing and as faith props. They are also very protocol minded in their approach because the Father is a law giver.

The Call Of The Son

These people tend to gravitate toward engaging the death and resurrection of Christ in their ministrations. They break evil legal strongholds and release souls from shackles and bondages on account of the blood of Jesus and His resurrection power.

The Call Of The Holy Spirit

These people move mightily in the Holy Spirit and His gifts. Their ministrations are confirmed by the mighty move of the spirit of God. There is instant healing and impartation of spiritual gifts.

THE FULL EXPERIENCE: BODY, SPIRIT & SOUL

May your whole spirit, soul and body be kept blameless at the coming of our Lord Jesus Christ.

The soul is your spirit being, made up of your spiritual genotype and phenotype.

The human spirit is not the same as the Holy Spirit. The human spirit is the substratum for spirits, including the Holy Spirit and familial spirits.

The body is an altar, a temple for spirits.

May we be sanctified through and through, in the name of Jesus.

Further reading: (1 Thes 5: 23, 1 Corin 6:19)

MINISTERING

There is an elementary teaching that appears to posit, people do not need anyone to pray for them. That they can access Jesus themselves. This is not solid food, it is milk. Even the Father works with the Holy Spirit and the Son, he dispatches angels and He works with humans.

The Law Of First Mention

In bible interpretation, there is a weight placed on the first time a role, word or title is mentioned. This is known as the law of the first mention.

The first time the word prophet appear in the bible, is in Genesis. Abimelech received divine instruction and direction through a dream to go to Abraham for prayers. In that vision Abraham was called a Prophet and his assignment was prayer/intercession. Based on the principle of the law of the first mention, a prophet's main task is to pray or intercede for people. Be it one-on-one , in secret or in the presence of others .

"Now therefore, restore the man's wife; for he is a prophet, and he will pray for you and you shall live".

Pray For You

People should be able to pray with you and also pray for you and over you, especially those who hold a five-fold ministry office in the kingdom and those you trust.

Is anyone among you sick? Let him call for the elders of the church, and let them pray over him, anointing him with oil in the name of the Lord.

❖ ❖ ❖

Isaac prayed to the LORD on behalf of his wife, because she was childless. The LORD answered his prayer, and his wife Rebekah became pregnant.

Jesus said, "Simon, Simon! Indeed, Satan has asked for you, that he may sift you as wheat.

But I have prayed for you, that your faith should not fail. Jesus prayed for Peter.

> *Jesus arose and is at the right hand of God, even making intercession for us.*

I have listed these few instances in order to cement the fact that one can and should be prayed for. Spiritual bondage and captivity start in the mind; we must renew our mind.

Imagine Abraham had not prayed for Abimelech; he may have ended up dead. (based on the instruction from the vision).

Imagine Isaac had not pleaded on behalf of Rebecca, there would not have been the nation Israel.

Imagine Jesus had not prayed for Peter; Peter would have been sifted as wheat. Peter went back fishing when Jesus died, he surely would need the intercession and intervention.

> Intercessors share in the Office of the Son who intercedes for us.

Further reading: (Gen 20:7, Heb 5:12-14, Jam 5:14-15, Rom 8:34, Gen 25:21, Lk 22:31-32)

GRADUATION SYSTEM

On a flight, the boarding pass grant access to the plane.

As to who sits in business, economy or first class it would depend on the price on the ticket.

Some Christians confuse access with position or seating.

Yes, the veil is torn, there is access. Now, the price you pay determines your seat in the spirit realm.

Jesus I Know And Paul I Know, Who Are You?

This episode occurs in the book of Acts when the seven sons of Sceva sought to cast out a demon in the name of Jesus. The demon possessed jumped on them. They were overpowered, wounded and stripped naked.

It is not merely mentioning the name of Jesus, it is about your seating and recognition.

◆ ◆ ◆

There was also a prophet, Anna at the time Jesus was born. It is written that she never left the temple but worshipped night and day, fasting and praying. She had been investing in prayer and consecrating herself for over fifty years. The point here is this; these titles of Prophet, Apostle etc come by investment of prayer, fasting, tutelage and learning through process. Recognition in the spirit realm comes with a price. The gift and grace of God is stewarded.

There are realms, dimensions, first, second, third heavens etc., glory realms, throne rooms, mansions, courts of heaven.

Anna committed and devoted herself to prayer. There are monks, priests, nuns, sisters who commit themselves daily to learning and studying about the things of God- spiritual knowledge is not the same as theological knowledge. Jesus called the fisherfolk, the unschooled and committed to these mysteries. Acts 4:13

Understand that people by exercising their gifts and investing themselves, may ascend dimensions that another may not be able to ascend or so easily receive from.

There is a journey to maturity in the knowledge of Christ. It is dangerous to not recognize that we are all at different stages of that journey and apprenticeship.

How far can you go? We all have different abilities, capacities, purposes and functions. Godly contentment is pivotal in harnessing the unique talents in God's kingdom. Leverage the strength of others in places that you cannot swim to.

Further reading: (Acts 19:13-16, Lk 2:36-37,1 Pt 4:10, 1 Corin 3:1-2, Rev 14:2-3, Heb 6:1- 3, Eze 47:4,5)

COMMON PRACTICES

The Greek word for spirit is *pneuma.* This gives an impression of breath or blow, air in motion.

Everyone breathes the same air, it is therefore not surprising that different religions and faiths share similar or common practices. These commonalities give credence to the existence of the supernatural and credibility to proven ways and protocols to access the realm.

Fasting

This is the abstinence from food, drink or pleasure for the purpose of religious or ethical reasons.

Muslims fast during what is called Ramadan, Christians fast, Buddhists fast, Hindus fast, Jews fast.

Silent Contemplation

All the major religions have reflective moments of silent contemplation. Example, Isaac would go to the field to meditate.

Further reading: (Gen 24:62-63)

Charity

This is the act of giving alms. All major religions encourage tending to the needy.

Prayer

This is the communication between humans and deity. All religions engage the supernatural via spoken words. Communication is normally a two way affair, the human speaks and the deity speaks.

Initiation And Rites Of Passage

These include ceremonies such as water baptism, shaving beard or leaving the beard, circumcision etc.

All major religions also have teachers, priests and leaders. These people play the role of teaching and guiding their household and others in the ways and creed of the faith.

These are just a few of the common practices.

DO YOU HAVE A MESSAGE?

(2 Sam 18:19-33)

"Why will you run, my son, since you have no news ready?"

There is this fascinating story that happens when David's son Absalom gets killed. Joab, who was the commander of David's Army felt, owing to the grave nature of the news, the right person to deliver that message was the Cushite.

But Ahimaaz who was also a messenger insisted he be sent on the errand, Joab conceded to his persistence and sent him out, but without a message.

Ahimaaz outran the Cushite and got to King David. But then he was asked to stand aside, until the Cushite arrived to deliver the message.

This story paints a picture of how people are called and assigned tasks, based on their capacity and nature of the task at hand.

Apostle Paul said the gospel of the Gentiles has been committed to him; the gospel to the Jews to Peter.

David comes to face Goliath with a message; he points to Saul how he had killed the bear and the lion. That was his message. What is your own message?

When one carries a message, ministry becomes organic and not a chore.

God will begin to work within you, your family. The sickness, the childhood trauma, running family issues. (Abraham was called to come out of his father's house, that place of comfort, idol worship and unfruitfulness) The problem that bedevil and takes our joy is the one that holds the key to our message.

It is often an inside-out work. It is the successes, also the hard lessons and how we healed. That is how we get our message. Why will you run my son, when you have no message?

Further reading: (Rom 11:13, Gal 2:7, 1 Tim 2:7, 1 Sam 17:34-36)

THE BELIEVER'S NAVIGATOR

The New Birth: Simon The Sorcerer

There was this man called Simon, who believed and even desired to operate in the gifts of the Holy Spirit. However, when his request was processed by Peter, certain hidden issues came to the fore.

Peter pointed, Simon's heart was not in the right place. According to Peter, Simon was full of bitterness and captive to sin.

Simon confessed and humbly asked that Peter pray for him to the Lord.

Simon the sorcerer believed, got baptised and even followed Philip everywhere. Yet there were issues within, that had to be dealt with. These came to the fore after the coming of the Apostles Peter and John.

On this faith journey in Christ, we have all come as we are, carrying all sorts of hurts, worries, trauma, yokes and bondages. Some issues we bring are physical, others spiritual.

Further reading: (1 Corin 12, Acts 8: 9-24)

❖ ❖ ❖

The Evangelists would invite everyone, regardless of their shortcomings. Jesus spoke to misfits, mingled with tax collectors and social outcasts. So it was also with Philip as he went about his evangelistic mission. All are welcome! This is only the first stage in the believer's journey. Some are also born into church, because of believing guardians or parents. It is still the first stage, they would have their own personal encounter along the way.

The second stage in the believers' navigation is their pastoring. **The Pastors** care, check up, follow up and make one feel welcomed to the faith. How this happens is that one finds themselves in a pastoral church, a caring church family.

In the third stage, **the Teachers** would teach them elementary doctrine. Here people are encouraged to read/learn the bible. They are taught to not forsake the gathering of the brethren, they are taught charity etc.

Then there is the **Prophetic stage**. At this stage in their christian walk, there is the experience of the prophetic anointing and exposure to the gifts of the Holy Spirit. People get told of their prophetic destinies and role in their families and the gospel. Here, people have insight into their calling and begin to explore their own spiritual gifts.

> Sometimes this navigation is spirit led. It may involve people moving churches. (sometimes through moving houses or via a stirring of their spirit making them uncomfortable in their local churches)

The **Apostle stage** is the place of groundedness, balance, processed faith and wisdom. Here Apostle-teachers give solid food. They teach about the discerning of spirits, dealing with besetting sins and other major blockages in the walk with Christ. At this stage, the goal is to maximise one's potential and measure up to the fullness of their abilities and purpose. The Apostle stage is the highest in terms of knowledge, understanding and wisdom in the things of the spirit. The church is built on the foundation of the apostles and prophets, Jesus Christ himself, the chief cornerstone. (Eph 2:20)

PREACHER'S PRIDE

Preacher's pride is a term used to describe the false sense of security and invincibility that is assumed because one has charge of a pulpit.

A sign of the calling is that fire inside, that passion, concern, that call to action. For instance when Moses came to the defence of the Hebrew slave, killing an Egyptian in the process, it was an indication that he had a call to deliver his Hebrew kindred.

> *Moses would go on to understudy Jethro for some time, in order to come back to the same Egypt to do divine bidding.*

The difference between fire for keeping us warm in winter, or for barbecue and the one causing bushfire is how tamed the fire is. Our fire must be harnessed in a way that makes it kindle in the right manner. It is dangerous to not build wisdom infrastructure around our passions, interests and assignments.

Take good care of your health, your diet and nutrition. *The perfect design and will for our lives is divine health not divine healing.*

Attend also to your own spiritual needs and your family's. Take the plank from your own eyes in order that you might see clearly to remove the speck in others.

Further reading: (Exodus 2:11-25, Mk 6:14-29, Matt 7:3-5)

PRAY FOR CHILDREN

Jesus admonished that the children be allowed to come to Him. He placed His hands on them, prayed for them.
Job, a righteous and upright man- the greatest of all the people of the East would sanctify his children. He would rise early in the morning and offer burnt offering on their behalf. Job did this

consistently.
Further reading:(Matt 19:14, Job 1:5)

THE YOUNG PROPHET AND THE OLD PROPHET

This is a story about a young Prophet from Judah, who received specific divine instructions not to eat, drink water or return by the same way he came, after he completes an assignment at Bethel.

He initially passed the test when King Jeroboam asks him to come home with him for food and reward.

However, he could not follow through with his divine script and perished as a result. He compromised and fell for deception from another Prophet who fabricated a lie that he had been sent by God to tell him to eat and drink, to bring him home for food.

The story teaches a lot, however I will emphasise just one theme, staying connected to the Source, the scriptwriter.

This story of the young prophet and old prophet is not about age. It is a status quo versus a new thing narrative.

In Exodus 6:2,3kjv the Lord said to Moses, that His name JEHOVAH was not known to his forebears Abraham, Isaac and Jacob. He specifically mentioned that He appeared to them as God Almighty, El Shaddai.

Here is this same God, ready to reveal another side of him to Moses. Sometimes He wants to do a new thing with us. New wine is not put in old wine skins.

It is likely that if David had put on Saul's apparel to face Goliath; he would have been killed, the same manner the young prophet lost his place in divine plot.

We are all original, made in the likeness of the Godhead to express and manifest a unique revelation of the creator. Don't lose your script, your originality, your authentic self, your true self. That was the error of the young prophet.

Stay true to the Source, fight the good fight, run the race, keep the faith, finish the course and take your crown. Amen!

Further reading: (1 Kgs 13, 1 Sam 17:38)

CONCLUSION

When the music fades
And all is stripped away

I'll bring You more than a song, For a song in itself
Is not what You have required

You search much deeper within through the way things appear
You're looking into my heart
It's all about You, all about You, Jesus

   --END

QR CODE FOR BOOKS

Please scan the qr code with the camera of your phone and the link to the amazon/lulu site to purchase warriors have wounds or Holistic will appear on the screen. Simply click on the link on your camera screen to take you to the site.

Holistic

Warriors Have Wounds

BOOKS BY THIS AUTHOR

Warriors Have Wounds

This book is an invitation to the table of lenity. It is a recognition that anyone who achieved anything faced some form of obstacle, pain, and hurt. Some even paid the ultimate price, with their lives. The wounds are a reminder, that we survived to tell the tale.

Holistic

In Holistic, the author seeks for us to break from limiting beliefs, thoughts and behaviour and to embrace change, growth, and transformation. The survival of the fittest is the survival of the fit for purpose.

Printed in Great Britain
by Amazon